D0626878

DON'TS FOR
MOTHERS

DON'TS
FOR MOTHERS

A. & C. BLACK, LTD.
LONDON

INTRODUCTION

If this book is to be of use to mothers and to the rising generation, as I humbly hope and trust that it will be, it ought not to be listlessly read, merely as a novel or as any other piece of fiction; but it must be thoughtfully and carefully studied, until its contents, in all its bearings, be completely mastered and understood.

I express the hope that my advice, through God's blessing, may not have been given in vain; but that it may be—one among many—an humble instrument for improving the race of our children—England's priceless treasures ! O, that the time may come, and may not be far distant, 'That our sons may grow up as the young plants, and that our daughters may be as the polished corners of the temple !'

ANON

DON'TS FOR MOTHERS

PREGNANCY AND CHILDBIRTH

DON'T indulge in any species of excess. Endeavour to keep the mind in the greatest tranquillity.

Don't indulge in the caprices of pregnancy to too great a degree.

Don't allow yourself to be tightly laced, this species of self torture fails of the desired effect and has pernicious consequences. Light and loose clothing is best for both mother and child.

Don't employ the common sort of female midwife. Their ignorance is the cause of many fatal accidents.

Don't allow delicacy to endanger. Engage the best female practitioner to be had, under the direction of a professional man, who should be in the house to apply to in the case of necessity.

Don't forget that in nineteen cases out of twenty no assistance whatever is necessary to a woman in labour, only good sense enough to leave nature to do her own work.

ABLUTION

DON'T bathe your new-born babe in *cold* water. It frequently produces stuffing of the nose or looseness of the bowels.

Don't, however, run into an opposite extreme. *Hot* water weakens and enervates the babe, and thus would predispose him to disease. Lukewarm *rain* water is the best to wash him with.

Don't feel it necessary to wash your infant's head with brandy.

Don't use the same sponge to bathe more than one infant. The promiscuous use of the same sponge is a frequent cause of inflammation of the eyes.

Don't use white lead as a powder. Some are in the habit of using it, but as this is a poison, it ought *on no account* to be resorted to.

Don't neglect the washing of creases made by the flesh of very fat children as the skin of these parts becomes sore and inflamed. Rose water or spring water is sufficient to prevent this inconvenience.

Don't allow a babe's clothes to become wet with urine. Children can be taught cleanliness, by putting a vessel under their lap when there is a sign of evacuation and will soon be not content to do without it. This practice may be begun at five or six weeks.

Don't neglect the morning wash. Cleanliness is one of the grand incentives to health, and therefore cannot be too strongly insisted upon. A child who is every morning well soused and well swilled with water seldom suffers either from excoriations or any other of the numerous skin diseases.

Don't let the babe remain for a long period in his bath. Let there be no dawdling in the washing, let it be quickly over.

DIET

Don't avoid the bosom. The infant ought to be put to the breast soon after birth, the interest of both the mother and child demands it.

Don't feed a new-born babe upon gruel. It disorders the bowels, causes a disinclination to suck, and thus makes him feeble.

Don't neglect to apply the child *alternately* to each breast. Sometimes, a child, for some inexplicable reason, prefers one breast to the other, and the mother, to save a little contention, concedes the point. And what is frequently the consequence ?—a gathered breast !

Don't have your baby constantly at the breast. This practice is injurious both to parent and to child.

Don't resort to broths. They are apt to turn acid on the stomach, and to cause flatulence and sickness, they, sometimes, disorder the bowels and induce griping and purging.

Don't forget to be sure that cow's milk is of good quality, if it must be given as a substitute. If you have not a cow of your own, have the milk from a *respectable* cow keeper.

Don't stuff a babe—never overload his little stomach with food, it is far more desirable to give him a little not enough, than to give him a little too much. Many a poor child has been, like a young bird, killed with stuffing.

Don't add either gin or oil of peppermint to the babe's food. It is a murderous practice.

Don't choose a wet nurse of a consumptive habit. Check if she or any of her family have laboured under "king's evil".

Don't employ a wet-nurse if there be any seams or swellings about her neck. She should have a plentiful breast of milk of good quality and good nipples, sufficiently long for the baby to hold.

Don't forget to assure yourself that the wet-nurse's own babe is strong and healthy, that he be free from a sore mouth, and, as nearly as possible, of the same age as your own.

Don't cram a wet-nurse with food and give her strong ale to drink.

Don't allow a wet-nurse to remain in bed until a late hour, and then continue in the house as if she were a fixture.

Don't let your wet-nurse succumb to fretting. She ought strictly to avoid crowded rooms ; her mind should be kept calm and unruffled. Nothing disorders the milk so much as passion and other violent emotions of the mind.

Don't give your child meat until he have several teeth to chew it with. But remember, meat ought to be given sparingly. Much meat is injurious to a young child.

Don't gorge the babe with food, it makes him irritable, cross and stupid; cramming him with food might bring on convulsions.

Don't keep your child from butter because you fear it is too rich for his stomach. Butter, in moderation, is nourishing, fattening and wholesome.

Don't allow your child luncheon. If he want anything to eat between breakfast and dinner let him have a piece of dry bread. He will never eat more of that than will do him good, and yet he will take sufficient to satisfy his hunger, which is very important.

Don't neglect to be sure a child eats salt with his dinner. Let a mother see that this advice is followed, or evil consequences will inevitably ensue.

Don't give your child beer with his dinner – this practice is truly absurd, and fraught with great danger! Not only so, but it is inducing a child to be fond of that which in after life may be his bane and curse.

Don't allow your child to take cakes or sweetmeats. Such things both cloy and weaken the stomach.

Don't keep your child from the table. A child ought to commence to dine with his parents as soon as he be old enough to sit up at the table. It makes him a little gentleman in a manner that nothing else will.

SLEEP

Don't attempt to harden a young child either by allowing him, in the winter time, to be in a bedroom without a fire, or by dipping him in cold water, or by keeping him with scant clothing on his bed. He ought to be kept comfortably warm.

Don't rock an infant to sleep, it might cause him to fall into a feverish, disturbed slumber, but not into a refreshing, calm sleep. Besides, if you once take to that habit he will not go to sleep without it.

Don't follow the practises of the Dutch or the French. The Dutch keep their infants in a state of repose, always rocking or jogging them. The French are perpetually tossing them about. A medium would be most favourable.

Don't put glaring colours, a lighted candle or anything that glitters opposite an infant's bed. The irritation is likely to cause inflammation of the eyes. Shades of green, grey and brown are preferable.

Don't leave foul linen, dirty vessels or remains of food in the infant's room.

Don't wake up your baby to show your friends what lovely eyes he has got; let them wait till he has had his sleep out.

Don't allow your baby to sleep upon your lap. This practice ought never to be countenanced. He sleeps cooler, more comfortably and soundly in his crib.

Don't let your baby sit up at night. Bathe him at the same time every day, and have him ready for bed by the time his father comes home from business.

Don't, upon any account, entrust your babe at night to a young and thoughtless servant. Young girls are usually heavy sleepers and are thus too much overpowered with sleep to attend to their necessary duties.

HEALTH

Don't use singed linen to wrap the navel-string ; it frequently irritates the infant's skin. There is nothing better than a piece of fine old linen rag, *unsinged*.

Don't hasten the separation of the navel string. It ought always to be allowed to drop off. Meddling with the navel string has frequently cost the babe a great deal of suffering, and in some cases even his life.

Don't use a pacifier. Its prolonged use is harmful, and is apt to be followed by thick misshapen lips, irregular teeth and a deformed palate.

Don't allow the infant's head to hang forward or fall back, like flowers too heavy on their stalks. It damages the spine and many infants suffer convulsions and other injuries.

Don't swathe an infant like an Egyptian mummy, this impedes the progress of nature.

Don't allow young infants to be offended by strong excitements. Guard against all loud and harsh noises, rough handling, powerful smells and pungent tastes.

Don't fear the vaccination of your child. It is one of the greatest blessings ever conferred upon mankind. Small-pox, before vaccination was adopted, ravaged the country like a plague, and those who did escape with their lives were frequently made loathsome and disgusting objects by it.

Don't prevent your child from the sucking of his thumb. It will often make a cross infant contented and happy, and will frequently induce a restless babe to fall into a sweet refreshing sleep.

Don't give a child who is teething either coral or ivory to bite as it tends to harden the gums. Softer substances, such as a piece of wax taper, or an India-rubber ring, or a piece of the best bridle leather, or a crust of bread, are of great service.

Don't assume that your baby is obliged to have trouble when teething. A healthy child ought to have no more trouble cutting his teeth than in growing his hair.

Don't purge an infant during teething or any other time. IF WE LOCK UP THE BOWELS, WE CONFINE THE ENEMY, AND THUS PRODUCE MISCHIEF.

Don't allow your babe to look at the glare either of a fire or lighted candle, as the glare tends to weaken the sight, and sometimes brings on an inflammation of the eyes.

Don't physick your family with too much frequency. It is an unnatural thing to be constantly dosing a child with medicine.

Don't kiss your infant on the mouth. Diptheria, tuberculosis and syphilis have often been communicated in this manner. Infants ought never to be kissed except on the forehead, and even that should be seldom permitted.

Don't make a practice of standing *behind* your baby to address him. In speaking to, and in noticing a baby, you ought always to stand *before* him, or it might make him squint.

Don't confuse or distract the babe. His soul, like his body, is weak and require but little sustenance at a time. Gentleness, patience and love are everything in education.

Don't over stimulate the babe, a multitude of new playthings will only serve to confuse him.

Don't treat the mind of the babe like that of a mature and rational being.

Don't forgo the daily inspection of your child's diapers. A mother ought daily to satisfy herself as to the stage of the bladder and bowels of her infant.

Don't attempt to treat serious diseases without the assistance of a medical man. The ailments and diseases of children, such as may, in the absence of the doctor, be treated by a parent, are the following :—Chafings, Convulsions, Costiveness, Flatulence, Gripings, Hiccup, Looseness of the Bowels, Dysentery, Nettle-rash, Red-gum, Stuffing of the Nose, Sickness, Thrush.

Don't, unless it be violent, interfere with a bleeding from the nose. It is frequently an effort of Nature to relieve itself and ought not to be restrained.

Don't allow too sedentary a life. Look at those children employed in manufactories, whose sallow looks and sunk eyes the heart shudders to behold.

Don't oblige a child to take exercise directly after a full meal. The best time for taking exercise is before meals.

Don't be afraid if your daughter should acquire masculine habits, or rough manners. As growing children they should have free use of their limbs and are likely to be the most graceful and healthy in adulthood.

Don't accuse a child of pretending to be ill; false accusation may augment the child's disease and, if it be just, a punishment ought to follow, which would be better avoided.

Don't let visitors see a sick child; they will only excite, distract and irritate him, and help to consume the oxygen of the atmosphere; a sick-room, is not a proper place, either for visitors or gossips.

Don't select a sick-nurse who is either too old or too young. If she be old she is often garrulous and prejudiced ; if she be young, she is frequently thoughtless and noisy ; therefore choose a middle-aged woman.

Don't disturb the stillness of a child's sick-room. Creaking shoes and rustling silk dresses ought not to be worn in sick-chambers.

CLOTHING

Don't weigh your infant down with long and cumbersome clothing. For clothes to reach to the ground, when the child is carried about, is foolish and cruel in the extreme.

Don't, where possible, use pins in the dressing of your child. Make diapers with loops and tapes, and thus altogether supersede the use of pins in the dressing of an infant. If pins be used, they ought to be the Patent Safety Pins.

Don't put clothes on your babe that are warm from the fire.

Don't neglect to give a child clean clothes daily. Where this cannot be afforded, the clothes, as soon as they are taken off at night, ought to be well aired so as to free them from perspiration.

Don't insist upon caps. A child is better without caps ; they only heat his head, cause undue perspiration, and thus make him more liable to catch cold.

Don't constrict your child in tight clothing. The clothing of a child, more especially about the chest, should be large and full in every part, and be free from tight strings.

Don't allow children to wear tight bands round their waists, it is a truly reprehensible practise.

Don't cover your child's head with felt, or with any thick impervious material. It is a well-ascertained fact that beaver and silk hats cause men to suffer from headache, and to lose their hair— the reason being, that perspiration cannot possibly escape through them

Don't permit a child to be in the glare of the sun without a hat. If he be allowed, he is likely to have a sun-stroke, which might either at once kill him, or might make him an idiot for the remainder of his life.

Don't allow your child to wear tight shoes. They cripple the feet, causing corns and bunions and interfere with the proper circulation of the foot. In the article of shoes you ought to be particular and liberal.

Don't leave off your child's winter clothing until the spring be far advanced : allow the winter clothes to be worn until the end of May.

Don't regard fashion over health in the matter of your child's dress. The present fashion is absurd. The boys go bare-legged ; the little girls are dressed like women, with their stuck out petticoats, crinolines, and low dresses !

Don't dress children as men and women, dress children as children.

Don't allow a child's clothing to be anything other than plain, light and warm. All kinds of ornaments and finery are injurious to their health.

Don't put boys into trowsers too young but keep them in petticoats until they are four years old. Never put trowsers on girls at all.

Don't allow a girl to dress with frivolity; it does great mischief to both fortune and character; but want of neatness and want of taste are particularly disgusting.

Don't use stays on your daughter.
These are the origins of a thousand
deformities and diseases, and the cause
of many fatal accidents. Tight lacing
squeezes and torments, and whatever
hurts the health produces ugliness.
Why should a waist be pinched until it
is as small as an arm?

Don't talk about dress but be careful
always to have your own dress neat and
well-fitted, and show a delicate and pure
taste in the choice of colours. By these
means, children will form the habit of
dressing well.

IN THE NURSERY

Don't establish a nursery without a water-closet near at hand. If this be not practicable, the evacuations ought to be removed as soon as they are passed.

Don't allow a motion to remain for any length of time in the room. It is a filthy and idle habit in a nurse-maid.

Don't allow your child to touch or play with the fire ; frightful accidents have occurred from mothers and nurses being on these points lax.

Don't permit your child to sit with his back to the fire; it weakens the spine and thus his whole frame; it causes a rash of blood to the head and the face, and predisposes him to catch cold.

Don't have your nursery wall covered with green paper--hangings. Green paper hangings contain large quantities of arsenic—arsenite of copper (Scheele's green)—which, I need scarcely say, is a virulent poison, and which flies about the room in the form of powder.

Don't hang the nursery walls with paintings of bad quality. The horrid daubs and bad engravings that usually disfigure nursery walls are enough to ruin the taste of a child.

Don't put down a carpet in your nursery. A carpet harbours dirt and dust, which dust is constantly floating about the atmosphere, and thus making it impure for him to breathe.

Don't make the bed of a child either very hard nor very soft. Extremes should be avoided in nourishment, clothing and beds. Feather beds should be denied them.

Don't make a hasty decision in the choice of his nurse. She should be steady, lively, truthful, and good tempered ; and must be free from any natural imperfection, such as squinting, stammering &c.,

Don't permit a nurse to tell her little charge frightful stories of ghosts and hobgoblins; if this be allowed, the child's disposition will become timid and wavering, and may continue so for the remainder of his life.

Don't allow anyone to punish your child by putting him into a dark cupboard or cellar; your child should never know fear.

Don't allow your nurse to use a perambulator. They are very apt to make a child stoop, and to make him both crooked and round-shouldered. Also, those perambulators are dangerous in crowded throughfares. They are a public nuisance.

Don't let your child put on airs with the servants. Teach him to be always polite. Snobbery begins in the nursery.

Don't always be telling your child how wicked he is ; how God will never love him, and all the rest of such twaddle ! Rather, find out his good points and dwell upon them, praise him where and whenever you can, and make him feel that, by perseverance and blessing, he will make a good man.

AMUSEMENTS

Don't restrain your child from romping in the nursery. It is his castle, and he should be Lord Paramount therein.

Don't suppress noise. If he choose to blow a whistle, or to spring a rattle, or make any other hideous noise which to him is sweet music, he should be allowed to do so. If any members of the family have weak nerves, let them keep at a respectful distance.

Don't, on any account, allow him to sit any length of time at a table, amusing himself with books, &c; let him be active and stirring. He ought to be tumbled and rolled about to make the blood bound merrily through the vessels.

Don't let your nurse dress for fashion. The present race of nurses are so screwed in with tight stays (aping their betters) that they are not able to stoop properly for romps with their charge.

Don't let your child write with one elbow on the table. One shoulder will inevitably become higher than the other if they acquire this habit.

Don't send your child out to walk in a fog ; he will, if you do, be almost sure to catch cold. It would be much safer to send him out in rain than in fog, though neither the one nor the other would be desirable.

Don't keep your child in during winter. Provided he be well wrapped up, the cold will brace and strengthen him. Cold weather is the finest tonic in the world.

Don't neglect a toy. The best toy for a child is a box of unpainted wooden bricks, which is a constant source of amusement to him.

Don't make Sunday a day of gloom. Of all the days in the week, Sunday should be the most cheerful and pleasant. You can no more make a child religious by gloomy asceticism, than you can make people good by Act of Parliament.

Don't hold children's parties. They are one of the great follies of the present age ; where children are dressed up like grown-up women, stuck out in petticoats, and encouraged to eat rich cake and to drink wine, and to sit up late at night ! Their pure minds are blighted by it.

Don't neglect the educative possibili-
ties of the stamp collecting mania. A
youth may become quite an authority
on geography through this pastime. He
will pour over an atlas in the way some
boys would with a book of adventure.

BOYHOOD AND GIRLHOOD

DON'T, on any account, allow your child to do at one time what you have forbidden him at another.

Don't punish a child from the selfish motive of indulging your own bad passions.

Don't punish a child too harshly. A punishment should always be as mild as it can be. Small children may be sent to bed without supper or tied in an arm-chair, or sent out of the room and forbidden to return, &c.

Don't trust a child again for some time if he abuse your confidence.

Don't undertake to make a child do a thing unless you are very sure you can make him do it. Once instance of successful resistance to authority will undo the effects of a year's obedience.

Don't suffer a child to be accused of a fault until you are perfectly aware he has been guilty of it.

Don't forget to tell a child *why* you are punishing him. If you do not he will never learn what behaviour offends.

Don't attempt to manage a boy if he is too bad to be governed by any other means than a flogging: tell his father of his disobedience and request him to punish the boy.

Don't use the whip frequently; flogging should only be resorted to in a child in whom evil feelings have become strong and when the wrong thing has been done over and over again, and when gentler punishments fail.

Don't object to a father's punishing a child when he thinks proper; at least not before the child.

Don't degrade a child—bringing a child into a room before strangers, wearing a foolscap or some bad name fastened upon them is not healthy for the character.

Don't allow a child to stay home from school if he is good; this gives him the idea that going to school is a task.

Don't offer money as a reward for doing right. Avarice thus encouraged and this is more contemptible and injurious to the character.

Don't allow wastefulness and prodigality. Teach children to be economical.

Do not allow a child to do what the father has forbidden, sewing discord.

Don't show a child the habits of carelessness, such as leaving things lying about, blotting books &c. Defects of this sort are the origin of numerous evils and many a failure in business or disordered household may be traced back to the indulgence of these habits in early life.

Don't overlook a single instance of carelessness. If a little girl cannot find her gloves, or bonnet, when about to take a walk then oblige her to stay at home.

Don't gloss over trifling deceptions with excuses; speak of them with unlimited abhorrence and contempt.

Don't commit those errors in early management that then leads to children being possessed with the idea that they may have everything. A child properly managed will seldom ask twice for what you have told him he should not have.

Don't tell untruths, if children want something improper do not tell them it will bite. It is not true and the smallest child will soon lean to disbelieve you.

Don't inspire a terror of animals, such as beetles, mice, spiders &c. Children would never have fear of animals unless it were put into their heads.

Don't frighten your child by filling their minds with terrific images of mysterious ideas of something harmful in the dark.

Don't be cruel and add another suffering if tears are not occasioned by pain. A child may usually be pacified by stroking a kitten or patting the dog.

Don't point out faults with an air of triumph or ridicule, so as to create irritation and dislike.

Don't discourage questions but, at the same time, children must be taught that they cannot *always* be attended to.

Don't lie. If a question is asked that is beyond experience refer the child to his father.

Don't praise too much for a child's quickness, or their wit. This leads to asking a number of pert, useless questions and should be promptly and decidedly checked. It is the germ of vanity and affectation.

Don't encourage a child to show off before company. The habit of reciting verses and displaying acquirements before strangers is the worst of all possible things for children.

Don't allow a child to form a habit of staying in the kitchen; not on account of any difference in station but because domestic staff change frequently and a parent is often uncertain as to their habits and principles.

Don't allow a child to give their attention exclusively to one thing. They will become careless and unobserving about everything else and impair general usefulness.

Don't encourage children to speak rudely, or make unnecessary demands on the domestic staffs' time and patience.

Don't teach a child to observe and respect the feelings of others for the sake of making themselves pleasing, but because it is kind and benevolent to do so.

Don't place disproportioned or badly drawn pictures into the hands of children. Good taste is of less consequence than good feelings and pictures have an important effect in forming their taste.

Don't keep creatures as pets, that must be confined in cages and boxes; no pleasure can be good which is so entirely selfish.

Don't allow a child to be excused from finishing what she has begun. The custom of having half a dozen things on hand at once should not be tolerated.

Don't neglect habits of perseverance. Even in so small a thing as untying a knot, a boy should be taught to think it unmanly to be either impatient or discouraged.

Don't allow children, particularly girls, to read anything without parental consent.

Don't encourage an exclusive and injurious taste for fiction in girls. Allow the occasional perusal of novels which are pure in spirit and in language.

Don't exaggerate a fault or dwell unnecessarily upon it. Dwell less on the individual offence than on the deep fountain of depravity with the child.

Don't allow the child to whine and fret, as there is nothing worse for the health. Habits of discontent develop chronic diseases and a peevish child has little chance of growing up healthy or happy.

Don't lock up a child in a dark room, or inflict any other punishement which may affect their nerves. A child frequently exposed to such debilitating feelings can never become so robust in body or virtuous in mind as he might otherwise have done.

Don't, however, fall for the palpable absurdity that all children can be educated without coercion and that punishments are never resorted to. But the less they are used the better.

Don't allow thoughtless persons to amuse themselves by exciting the jealousy of a child. It leads to feelings of hatred and lays the foundations of moral depravity.

Don't talk over troubles around the
child, few things can be more hurtful
to the health than to see dismal counte-
nances and hear constant lamentation.

Don't allow the child to be with
persons who stutter, or have any
extraordinary sort of ugliness. However
great their merits in other respects they
are unfit to have the care of children
and should not be places as attendants
or instructors.

Don't allow children indiscriminate
and careless intercourse with strangers.
They may learn vicious and destructive
habits.

Don't allow children to sit crooked, leaning the chest against a table or acquiring any other awkward positions detrimental to health and beauty.

Don't oblige children to devote hours to study which ought to be employed in exercise in the open air. *Nothing* should interfer with air and exercise.

Don't, on any account, allow a boy to have a glass of wine after dinner. His young blood does not require to be inflamed, and his sensitive nerves excited, with wine.

Don't permit a youth to drink green tea. It is apt to make people nervous, and boys and girls ought not even to know what it is to be nervous.

Don't allow a boy much pocket money; if he be so allowed he will be loading his stomach with sweets, fruit and pastry, and thus his stomach will become cloyed and disordered.

Don't confine your youth within doors. Insist upon him taking plenty of exercise.

Don't coddle your boy; this is a rough world of ours and he must rough it. Poor youths who are, as it were, tied to their mother's apron strings, are much to be pitied; they are usually puny and delicate and utterly deficient of self-reliance.

Don't allow a girl to be idle. It ruins her complexion, and her face becomes of the colour of tallow. The reason why so many young girls of the present day are sallow, under-sized and ill-shaped is for the want of proper exercise.

Don't let your youth dine exclusively on a fruit pudding or pastry. If he is to be healthy, strong and courageous, let him eat meat every day of his life.

Don't let your boy get into the habit of muttering. Youths often speak indistinctly from carelessness. Make him repeat his remarks distinctly. A course of lessons in elocution is an excellent cure. Note that muttering is sometimes a symptom of incipient deafness.

Don't try to keep your boys and girls in ignorance of the facts of life. They may remain innocent without being ignorant.

Don't crowd about a girl if she faints. Lay her flat upon her back and throw open the windows.

Don't allow horse exercise to supersede walking. However it is a splendid exercise; it strengthens the chest, it braces the muscles and gives energy and courage. Riding is both exercise and an amusement, and peculiarly suitable for the fairer sex, as their modes of exercise are somewhat limited.

Don't permit a youth to play the flute, blow the bugle or any other wind instrument. It is injurious to health; the lungs and windpipe are brought into unnatural action by them.

Don't be disappointed when you learn that 'it' is a girl and not a boy. Don't let that disappointment tinge your treatment of your girls. A girl is every bit as important to this world as a boy.

Don't fill up the time of female children with the cultivation of *accomplishments*. These are a smattering of ornamental, but useless, arts and fill up the time of children without adding much to their physical and moral welfare. A cheerful temper is a better quality.

Don't suffer the mind to brood over the external distinctions of society. Neither seek nor avoid those who are superior in fortune; meet them on the same ground as you do the rest of your fellow creatures and your children will do the same.

Don't neglect arithmetic, book-keeping and penmanship with girls. Should your daughter have an estate to settle or a household to run these are invaluable skills.

Don't strengthen a restless, roving tendency in a boy by accounts of remarkable voyages and adventures.

Don't countenance by word or example that silly affected sensibility which leads people to faint or run away at the sight of danger or distress.

Don't forget that the education of your child is never finished. Half the character is formed after we cease to learn lessons from books.

Don't hesitate to share domestic cares with daughters once they are old enough. When a girl is nine or ten years old she should be accustomed to doing her own making and mending.

Don't disregard a school as a method of instructing a daughter but do not trust a young girl at boarding school without being sure that her room-mate is discreet, well-principled and candid. It is better to have her mind a little less improved than to have her heart exposed to corrupt influences.

Don't put children off with lies, or further excite their curiosity by mystery and embarrassment if delicate subjects are raised. Mothers are the only proper persons to convey such knowledge to a child's mind.

Don't treat any member of the family who happens to have any peculiarity or personal defect with anything other than unusual delicacy and affection. A child will lose consciousness of the peculiarity if this rule is followed.

Don't show a preference for the smartest or prettiest child. This is exactly the reverse of right.

Don't encourage your daughter to attend balls. They induce young ladies to sit up late at night ; to dress too lightly ; and thus, thinly clad, they leave their homes for a suffocating hot ballroom. Their partners, the brilliancy and the music, excite their nerves to unnatural action and what is the consequence ? Fatigue, weakness, hysterics and extreme depression.

Don't shy away from talking to your daughter at this growing-up time. She needs to be told of the wondrous power of a young woman, and of how she stands for so much if she is only strong for goodness and purity.

Don't allow your daughter to become great friends with a man until she knows something about his home, how he is to his own people, where he spends his evenings and how he keeps Sunday.

Don't allow a youth to take lessons in singing before you have ascertained there be no disease of the lungs.

Don't make a fine lady of your daughter, or she will become puny and delicate, listless, and miserable. Let her be self-reliant and wait upon herself.

Don't put your youth to a light indoor trade, if he be delicate. The close confinement of an in-door trade is highly prejudicial to health. An out-door calling is advised, such as that of a farmer or tanner. They are seldom known to die of consumption.

Don't tax the intellect of a precocious child. A greater quantity of arterial blood is sent to the brain of those who are prematurely talented which may excite and feed inflammation, and convulsions or idiocy may follow should the precocious brain be overworked.

Don't allow your son to smoke. It is one of the most injurious and deadly habits a young man can indulge in. It contracts the chest, weakens the lungs and impairs the stomach. It debilitates the brain, stunts the growth, and is one cause of the present race of pigmies. It makes the young lazy and disinclined for work. It is one of the greatest curses of the present day.

Don't confine your daughter to fancy work and the piano. Mothers of England, let me entreat you, rescue your girls from the bondage of fashion and folly.

Published 2011 by A & C Black
Copyright © A & C Black, 2011
Bloomsbury Publishing PLC
49–51 Bedford Square
London
WC1B 3DP

ISBN 9781408152232

A CIP catalogue record is available for this book
from the British Library.

Printed by WKT Company Ltd, China